To Ted

all th

Be we

ure.

fou

Ur g

An Emptied Space

Best wishes

Mel.

An Emptied Space

Mel McEvoy

First published 2012
by Mudfog Press
c/o Arts and Events, Culture and Tourism,
P.O. Box 99A, Civic Centre, Middlesbrough, TS1 2QQ
www.mudfog.co.uk

Edited by Pauline Plummer for Mudfog Press
Cover Design by turnbull.fineart@btinternet.com

Print by EPW Print & Design Ltd.

ISBN: 978-1-8995039-2-6

Mudfog Press gratefully acknowledges
the support of Arts Council England
and Middlesbrough Council.

Acknowledgements

Poems from this collection have appeared as Editors'
picks on poetrycircle.com. It is a contemporary poetry
forum. One poem appeared in the Catholic Gazette
magazine. 'The Tackle' won a Darlington poetry
competition.

I would like to thank the poets and editors on Poetrycircle
for their continuous support and advice. A great deal of
thanks must go to Pauline Plummer who helped in
putting this collection of poems together.

Several of these poems are the result of encounters with
individuals in many situations during 30 years of nursing
in the North East. Names have been changed to protect
the identities of individuals. Many poems are reflections
on the last few days of life which is often hidden from
many of us. The single reason is to illustrate how we die
so we may have less fear.

This book is dedicated to my mother Mary McCormack
and my father Thomas McEvoy

Contents

Dying

Beginnings

New Skin

Tugged on the arm
by a mother's hand
from staring into
a cairn of coals
burning volcanic colours
behind a brass fireguard

from the world of toy-soldiers
lost in a battle
down the backs of sofas

from the dance
of a father's accent
telling of ghosts and the banshee's wailing.

Jerked from the skip
of pavement-flag games
to keep up with the pace
of other mothers in procession
towards the iron school railings.

A mother's grip
in a tight matted clench
wants a little longer
before she lets his hand slip.

At the end of the day
the school gate
releases a runner.
Within his littered pockets
among the marbles
and football cards
there's heat from
his throbbing fingers
about which he won't tell.

Unrequited Love on a Thursday Night

'Johnny, is your father coming yet
with the Giro?

Jimmy, have you got any money for me
before you go out?

What do you mean?
Of course it can't wait till next week.
The rent wants two weeks!
The red letters are in from the Gas and Electric.
They'll turn them off!
There'll be no milk or bread.

Well just fuck off then!
No! Jimmy give me some money!
Alright, before you go, look
at that poor bastard in the corner,
he's going to school
with the arse out of his trousers.
Other kids are laughing at him.
It's November.
He needs shoes
and he's got pumps on his feet.

I don't want to know
about your big schemes -
when this happens
when that happens.
It's all a load of shite.
In a hurry?
Can't wait can yea?
Can't wait to knock back the ale?
Starving for it aren't yea?
Going drink till yea vomit.

Managed to make it home?
Found the right house?
Singing are we?
Go to it when you want to do it.
Only had a pint, yea,
but you had to feed your mates as well!

A big man, 'let me get them in'
with no milk or bread in the house.
A big man: fucking Ladbrokes aren't yea?'

'Mary are you alright?
Have you hurt yourself?
Has he been the man again?
Are you still doing
the first reading at Mass on Sunday?
What's the beatitudes or something?
Is that God making promises?'

Growing up by the Ice Cream Van

The early evenings had their own Pied Piper
parading through the streets of the estate,
a beckoning jingle from Santangeli's ice cream van
calling to children to come running
with money from their mothers' purses.

The look in his eye seemed to suggest that he
was someone we knew or had known us as babies.
The big copper pennies, the silver six pence and
the half a crown were picked from hands
too small to reach the counter even standing on tiptoes.

Like a craftsman
he turned the cones carefully four at a time
letting the layers of thick white cream fall slowly
until we had a handful of snow capped mountains.
Then, he'd guide a red river of raspberry.

We came of age when our elbows
were able to rest on his counter and peer in at him
to discover the secrets of this
uncle to us all; smaller than normal
who looked taller because of the van.

The motor that whisked the cream rattled.
He twisted one of its parts with a white cloth.
The music lost bits off its tune and his gentle eyes
became uneasy keeping guard for sly,
long arms reaching into the boxes of cones.

The faces that once crowded the window
now kept a deliberate distance,
wanting the suck of cigarettes but
always eyeing the flake of the Ninety-Nines
being handed over to younger hands.

Caught the Grass Whispering

In the early hour
you find again a space
where the earth is soft and moist,
to stand alone on waste land
of coal-green grass,
in an amber mist of sodium,
between industrial plants.

At the edges of the waste land
barbed sharp stars twisted in rows
age reddish-brown from the rain
and camouflaged chemicals.

The fences split
a mitotic council estate
from the industrial complex.

This free patch of earth
is now for sale to planners
backs arched in bright waterproofs
gazing through a theodolite
at the field that was
Goodison Park, Anfield, Wembley
and Mexico City during the World Cup.

Jumpers were goal posts
for George Bests and white Peles.
Shoes for school went bare at the toes,
knees scraped, sweat darkened shirts.

Beyond the field
in the allotment jungle
adventures burst forth.
Ditches were jumped,
trees hugged and
grasshoppers hunted with shelled hands.

Frogs, like Buddhas,
watched us watching them,
ballooning their throats.
Jars with jam still on the rim
were brought for the black-spotted jelly.
The keen eyes that discovered the spawn
watched it grow tails and ripple
on bedroom windowsills.

Tarzan cries were heard all the evening
from the muscular Horse Chestnut, Larch and Ash trees.
Monkeys in school uniforms
dangled from tugboat ropes.

Branches became rifles,
bows and arrows
and sub-machine guns
with the propelled rattle of tongues.
German and British armies
were besieged, blown up,
slaughtered and resurrected
after school the next night.

It lasted long after the sun set behind
the half-constructed National Giro Complex.
Mothers had to hitch their skirts up
to climb over fences
looking for muddied warriors
as the sky bled over them
towards the dark blue night.

Diving to hide in the long grass,
betrayed by finger pointing friends,
protests silenced by a quickly aimed hand
and as ladders ran up stockings caught on briers
like a pilgrim people
we'd climb the hill:
one body in the blackening night
going home to the estate.

These thoughts like ghosts
want a home to go to
on somewhere that is no longer.
The earth that received the weight of feet,
young bodies hiding still
with cheeks against the grass,
eyes closed, hoping not to be caught
is now beneath
a pale grey tarmac car park.

Family Life

An Empty Space Without a Window

You are
chasing me
around the shed
at the bottom of the garden,
never quite catching me,
just over my shoulder
getting nearer.
Then I run faster.
That's how Mam remembers
standing in the doorway
pregnant with Nuala.

You were trying to get me in
out of the meteors of hail stones.
With my hands on my head
I cried: 'the dash is getting me.'
You got fed up trying
ran in and bolted the door.

I'm forever caught
in that dash
of hail stones.

Behind the cracked glass
there's no one watching
over us playing.
In our house Novembers
are never hopeful
as the dark roams around
looking for mischief
in the early evenings.
A kitchen bulb is the only arm around us.
Bridget is eight
tasting the sweet
poisoned importance
of being mother.

You're playing Cinderella
in a frilly gauze dress,
twirling near an open fire,
curtain as a headdress:
as the clock strikes.

In the newspaper
it said we were playing a game.
I've removed the fire guard.
I'm throwing paper on the fire.
I'm nearly three and you are four.
Pages twisted tight
full of jumbled words
opening slowly as if to speak.

Behind a whispered thought
dad made up the story to avoid prison
but never escaped the sentence
condemned to search every day
for that place where
it never ever happened.
He said he had to do the weekly shop
but took the two older boys with him
to replace a broken window.
Mam can't see you from her hospital bed, having Nuala.

There has always been
a vague image of seeing you
reaching for something up on the mantelpiece;
it must have been our tomorrows.

The dress started to smolder
as it brushed near the hot coals in the grate.
Bridget heard you from the kitchen
the small red glow began to spread
quickly melting the gauze.
She grabbed and ran out with you
straight into the face of a merciless wind
having been told: 'Any trouble go to Margaret's.'

Dad, the crucified one,
sat at your bedside for twelve days
forever carrying a pane of glass up a hill.
He couldn't put sentences together
to tell himself or God what happened.
Asked Margaret the neighbour
to come in and tell Mam in hospital.
She looked at dad then Bridget,
"I'll do it but don't you ever blame her,
just remember those burnt hands."

In the emptiness
no one remembered Nuala
being brought home.

Mam who was never sick
laid on her single bed
brought downstairs
opposite the fire.
Once, I came down
the big stairs one at a time,
pushed the door open slowly,
on a living room in darkness,
ready to run, and waited
to hear the roared chorus:
'Get back to bed!'

From the grate a dark brownish light,
flickered shadows
on the wall beside her bed.
She wouldn't answer me,
a lifted and dropped look,
kept staring into the fire,
watching you from the doorway
chasing me around the garden shed.
Nuala, fast asleep at her breast.

On an either/or morning
she got up, dressed Nuala,
put her in the pram and went looking
for a place along the river Mersey
to step off and find you.
Somehow, found
a place where
you must have been
at the back of a quiet church.

Bridget bore the blame.
At school she vanished
into places where
she felt the warmth
of brightly painted flowers
on large sea smoothed stones.
She started nursing
but could see you
in her room at night
refusing to talk.
At nineteen
admitted to a mental unit
to see if drugs and ECT
would make you leave
or bring you back.

She went looking for you,
in the places you used to be,
cycling around the estate
in a night dress,
making a house
in the allotment shed.
Drugged to forget
she spent hours keeping
everyone safe
in the hospital day room.
Five years as an inpatient
fighting fires
with an 'if only' thought.

Forty years later
Bridget smothered the flames.
At the moment dad died
and we were gathered
around the hospital bed
watching and waiting
as he faded to find you,
she broke a window
with a stone of a sentence:
'He made me lie to the police.
There was no fire guard around the fire.'

Motherhood on Lime Street Station

I

A moment
on Liverpool's Lime Street Station
should have only recorded
the departure of a son
leaving for Lourdes
but instead revealed
a life time of longing.

Keeping her distance from the crowd
but longing for the attention
saved just for her, she waited.
The leprosy of the unloved
manifests itself
as feeling alone
in a crowed place.

No one should see
a mother's fear of losing
the only thing in her life.

Feeling this ache might be an omen
she turned away
from kissing a grown son now leaving.

When she thought no one was looking
she walked towards the exit
a ladder in her tights
and a hole in the sole of her shoe.

II

She had grabbed him often before
and pulled him to her chest,
still wriggling,
immune to his arguments.
She mocked exaggerated claims
on how late other kids came in,
how their mothers never
came looking for them:
'Mam you're embarrassing me!'

It felt like every night
for sixteen years
she kept an eye on the clock,
the darkness,
and his dinner in the oven,
scoured the estate after curfew,
asking kids his whereabouts
and roaring his name into the night,
always knew the best hiding places.
Her shadow grew angry
under one sodium street light then another
to make sure it was her hand
that dragged his collar.

III

She never knew
how to keep the lid on
her own boiling pan.
The house could be quiet
but never without a foreboding.
Often plates were smashed
from a great height
against a Belfast sink.

Arguments continuous
as the noise from furnaces
burning white flames.
Neighbours were too afraid
to knock on walls.
The coalman walking up our path
looking for money
convinced himself that it could wait.
Even the parish priest lacked faith,
missing out Molly's house this time.

Their life together mocked
the order of the eight letters
in the word marriage,
snarling dogs on chains
six inches from each other.

Both were fluent
in obscenities,
skilled butchers of the word.
When a knife of a phrase
found its place
it was turned one way
then another.

The fight wasn't over
until he dragged up
the prostituted ghost of her mother,
the biggest hole in the whole of Ireland.
A politician's son
a local GP's brother,
a land owner,
visited and appeared
to have a right of access.
She worked 'in service'
unsure if she knew
what was going on,
and 'No' was a word
she had a right to say.

Three children -
only the nuns knew the father,
she being one of them,
the others given to work
in the convent laundry or on a farm.

IV

Born in a cottage with a thatched roof
down a country lane,
her actual house is celebrated
on an Irish postcard sold
in the local shop.
Everyone knew but her
why she was raised by
her grandmother and uncle.

In the thirties she remembers
wondering why
when she came top
in religious studies
she never got her merit.

In the church aisle praying
the stations of the cross
the priest's candle went out.
She lifted her candle to help,
backed away from that
look of contempt
as he walked past to a child
further down the church.

In a playground,
skipping with a wealthy girl,
who went on to be a nun,
who watched and waited
for the best time said:
'I know what you are.'

Waiting for a reply like:
'the best at skipping
in all the school.'
'You're a bastard
and your big sister is your mother.'
Knew it wasn't nice
but didn't know what it meant.

In a crowded front room
everyone dressed in their best
for a wedding, including her,
cousins and aunties,
all making decisions
about her hair and
the dress to wear.
Then she wondered why
the noise had stopped
and the sound of cars faded.
Went outside to see no one
she was left behind,
the only one in the house
the whole day long.

V

Seventeen: the churning stomach,
the tightness in the chest,
and the rapid pounding
began to ease
as she finally looked behind
as her town's name
became omitted
from the signs on the road
out the window on the back of a bus,
coming in from the country to work
as an auxiliary nurse in Dublin.

Black and white movies
don't prepare the innocent
when it comes to knowing
if you've found love or not.
Met a man at a wedding,
got married without
the buzz of love
in any of their stories.
There was a job he wanted,
had a better chance with a wife.

Started with cups and saucers,
a few pans
and the clothes they stood up in.
Furniture came with the room.
The landlady had the right
to look through your things
when you weren't in.
Ten on the one floor sharing a toilet.
Five years on, never managed
to own a chair or a dresser.

Surprised how much
the skin stretches for the first time.
You'd think, 'how can anything live in there?'
Just turned the corner
on one of Dublin's streets
and a cyclist knocked her down.
Baby born premature.
Every day for six weeks
she visited the hospital
until one day a nurse
leaned out of a first floor window
and shouted out:
'Don't bother coming today,
the child's dead.'
Borrowed money to bury the child.
No one attended the funeral
but the hearse driver
and a grave digger.

Put the child
in an opened grave
with a stranger.

Making conversation in her lodgings,
she didn't know then
some people are like vultures
circling for something juicy.
Told small things to one
and the whole tenement knew.
She could hear her secret
being mumbled to others
outside her door.
She remembers being cold
on Christmas Day
with the gas cut off
and nobody came to call
to share anything.
No priests to be seen
this deep in the slums.
Shocked when she saw
a wealthy woman
walking in Phoenix Park
wearing a fur coat
feeding bread to the ducks
thinking: 'We would have eaten that.'

VI

Always anticipating
life would bite deep again
given the chance.
Wondering what she was doing
sat on a boat crossing the Irish Sea
pregnant and two children hugged close,
entering the unknown fog of England.
Tight to her chest
her world of wealth in a potato sack

following the dictates
of a husband's letter.
From one slum to another
muster strength
after another child came
into a one room basement
on the dock road.
She thought the people here
kinder and didn't pry as much.

Without warning
the Liverpool council
cleared the slums en masse
to a newly built council estate
not far from Aintree Racecourse.
Nervous when she was given
her first ever key
to her very own door.
How do you fill all that space
with nothing to put in it?
Three bedrooms,
slate floors and no curtains.
When he stepped in the hall
he had tears in his eyes
'We'll never go home now.'
She screeched back
'Don't talk through your arse.
Go home to what?
We never had a home to go home to.'

In a Liverpool hospital, alone
after pushing out Nuala,
her seventh child,
she knew something wasn't right.
Too early for visiting,
she saw him through the window
standing outside the room
avoiding her eye,
not wanting to see the new baby.

He had been crying
but instead of him coming in
Margaret the neighbour
from across the street
came in without him
to tell her Joany, her four year old
had died from severe burns.
Up and out of bed within minutes
to see with her own eyes her child,
but the priest said don't go in
better to remember her how she was.
Returned home and stared for months
into the fire, asking.
Thought suicide must be easier,
cried, argued, got up
and pushed the pram again.

It is going to be different this time,
going to be stronger,
should never have left her with him.
Committed to be tight, close,
so they can't breathe without me.
I need them to all sleep with me.
With a tight hand-chain of children
she'd shop in a big supermarket.
Suddenly a hand clenched
around the emptiness
of a missing hand,
quickly she'd roar
in the crowded shop 'Nuala!'
Her daughter shamed,
circled through the aisles
came up behind her
and tugged, whispering
'Mam, stop shouting. I'm only here.'

VII

Never once looked long enough
in the mirror to have any style.
Gave up trying to squash
into tight elastic corsets.
Never used make-up or scent.
Never bought attractive clothing.
Wore out a hundred overalls in
fourteen years behind the local bar.
Never bought an item of jewellery,
lost original wedding ring to a
pawn-broker in Dublin
soon after marriage.

Uncomfortable with gifts,
silenced by remembered birthdays.
Her parish priest had a different
date for when she thought she was born.
Frozen by a son's warm embrace.
Soles of shoes had to move like
a mouth before ending up in a bin.

Remembered
every neighbour's child's name,
knew who came from where,
was married to whom
and where they were finally buried.
Went to anyone's help
at the first sign of need,
always making sandwiches at funerals.

At the same time
she felt pulled and chased.
It seemed
if she stopped long enough
something would catch up
and devour her.

Even now
the arguments run after her
in the small hours of the morning.

When her son returned
from this journey
he never told anyone his arrival time,
just appeared quietly at the kitchen door.
She was in the middle of
an intense conversation
with herself,
at the same time
turning sausages in a pan.
The door was open
and he watched her silently for a while
and then in a whisper said
'I love you.'
She quickly turned and
for the first and only time
he thought he saw
an unguarded face.
It stunned him;
he was looking
at a three year old
with arms raised
to be picked up
held and taken to the wedding.

The Price of Bus Fares

There are
patterned prints from boots
stamped into the tanned soil
in a slow stroll
the length of the furrows.

The potato drills
like lined paper
arrive after acres to where
the earth discreetly dips.

The river Shannon,
close, listened to, flows in stories,
curves and mounts upon currents wild,
waltzing, swaying
the bent and bowing reeds.
On stiller days the river
frowns and relaxes.

In gatherings blackthorn
meshes the blackbird.
The damp sharp scent of peat
rides with the breeze
the land's own breath.

A curlew's canticle drifts in the air.

Standing on the platform of a back loader
in a uniform crossed at the chest
with leather straps
chained to a machine and money bag,
the owner of such memories
guards a Liverpool corporation bus.

This role strips the Celt to a mere accent.
He daily walks the passages between seats
collecting fares or recollecting.
Visions of the life left
unroll like the tickets from the machine.
There are no rogue potatoes between the seats,
no earth either.

On days free from work
the iron-railed allotment gate
is opened.

In the middle of a square plot of dug land,
mid-furrow he stands
in old, mud splashed
bus trousers and boots,
a sail of a white shirt
sleeves wrung, rolled above the elbows,
grinning.

Spit fired and rubbed into coarse hands,
once the wooden handle of the instrument is gripped
back bent and straightening
the motion begins.
No longer a conductor but
a man carving the earth.

The grin on his face
is because he is
among memories
on an ancient bog.
In his mind a stuttering gig of a tune hops.
Whispers run through the woods.
The Shannon slows and its banks breathe in
and squeeze the salmon into the air…

Somewhere a curlew calls out.

'Come home ya fool….
Come home ya foool…
Come home ya fooool…'

Digging Deeper

My father's bogman's hands
tossed us free like pigeons.
We fled the captivity
of a council estate to soar,
make nests in the jungles of warlords
in the rouge of summer evenings
on his allotment.

I walked the cinder path
towards a father digging
out last year's crop of potatoes
to show him his growing grand daughter
adrift on the clouds of sleep.

A small boy races out
from a hole in the hawthorn hedge
carrying a lemonade bottle
bare legs moving
like piston shafts in full throttle,
scratched from getting deep
into the blackberry bush
where the juicy ones hide.

Stopped by the impact
of a large heavy rusted barrel,
a copper tap
like a periscope
sticking out above it,
he climbs into the mouth
of the circled rim,
hands holding on the edge,
feet off the ground,
looks, hesitates and buries his head
deep below the cold silky surface,
face clenched against the need for air,

determined to count slowly
up to twenty.
Eyes wide open
and blurred
into murky depths
where hid a pirate's treasure.
He pulls himself out after twenty five,
Grinning, swishing the chilled water
from his soaked head
now a real crimsoned pirate like Burt Lancaster.

A father's Irish rumblings
reach him like an arm
across the allotment
telling him to hurry
with the drink.
Now the Olympic Games -
David Hemery in the 400 meters hurdles,
Mexico 68, Coleman, the commentator,
blessing himself with most of the water
as he runs, crosses the tape
at a giant's feet,

noticing how calm he is here.
There is no roaring.
Is it the trees' soothing sounds?
A half-moon grin on his face,
he inspects the potatoes,
tells me their names
counts the drills
sinks the spade.

Walking through this past,
the knee high blades of grass
leave a trodden-down
trail to the present.
I bend my head and enter
a musty tool shed,
the door hanging on one hinge.

I lay down my little girl
to sleep among
an army of odd Wellington boots.
I wrap her up
as she turns in her sleep
in one of his old coats
folding its empty arms.

Walking towards him
wondering if he needs me
to run to the tap.
He stands like
a monolith
his boots buried
beneath the soil,
leaning one arm across
'the lugs' of the spade.

He has been watching me,
the soil behind him
dug over into a darker tan.
Drawing closer
to the jam jar glasses
I enter into his glance.
It seems he has just been
where I have been.
We embrace
remembering
us together,
on this piece of earth.

The Tackle

I turn around and walk
back to a playing field
to find a child getting ready
for a pub's under 11's football match.

I feel him wriggle his toes
inside his brother's boots
that needed extra socks to fit,
silencing their tongues with laces tied tight.

He stands on the wing bewildered,
occupied by their aggressive arguments
until the ball comes and he breaks away,
furious running towards goal.

The ball is kicked like a punch
unstoppable up in the top corner.

Twenty years on
I turn again and walk in on
angry parents still accusing
each other of past injustices.

It's the tackle from behind you least expect.

My Mother's Bag

was always as close -
under the table, beside the chair
at the bottom of the bed -
as the heart is that goes unnoticed.

Anything important
significant or precious
found its way deep into the bag.

Visits home always meant
several attempts at leaving.
She wouldn't let go
until she conceded with

'Get me the bag.'
Made the moment private
pulled out cash for petrol
and 'a little something for the kids.'

Just before she died
she sat up and said 'It is all over.
Get my bag. They have all gone.
Joany's gone, what is there to stay for?'

Days before her funeral
I climbed into a quiet moment
desperate to discover what sort
of service she wanted.

With her bag beside me
I opened it nervously
longing for her return,
for the feel that was her

and found many 'order of service',
the requiem masses of all her friends
and wrapped in an elastic band
three letters I'd written decades earlier.

Looking for Her Mam

I

Nuala's home-coming found no welcome waiting,
wrapped safe in a sheet tight as a shroud,
carried into a home still aching
into the shadows of curtains drawn.

Forever together in the one sentence,
from tender talk of features above a pram's hood
to a hushed descent into guarded stories
about Joany, and how she died.

How did you ever keep a float
in such waters
when no one had hold of you?
Too painful for nursery rhymes;
breast taken from mam lost in a storm.

Only found in photos when a new sister
appears. Never the focus of a camera
even in her first communion dress,
emphasis on a little sister, in a pretend one.

II

Every Friday for six years
you drove between rush hours
from Manchester to Liverpool
the distance from worry to relief,

the whole day warming the chair
next to a bed-bound mother.
Constant stream of reminiscence
still alive in the wide open space of the moment.

'Leaving?' she'd say in the way only
mothers to daughters can.
'I am going to buy you a cake
with hello and good bye on it.'

III

Gathered around the hospital bed waiting
for the last breath to stop coming.
I felt that when it did she'd entered
into a place somewhere else.

In the emptiness between death and the funeral
a grand daughter dreamt she saw her sat up
in the hospital bed, a cup of tea in her hand
saying: 'The pain's gone. I'm glad it's all over.'

The youngest daughter in all the photos
dreamed she was running, long hair flowing,
saying I have been looking for this feeling all my life
with a radiance that entered into her like the heat off an iron.

Nuala, you put on our mother's big coat
stood over the mound of earth
held our mother's bag in an elbow's crook
in the way she used to and still no dream,

only a sudden stiff neck that you got
on the night out mother died.
So at the reception, moving like a cripple,
you'd listen to tales about our mother.

What you noticed most in the last weeks
was the gradual absence of phone calls.
For years she'd call at least three times a day.
You sensed not phoning was a forewarning.

IV

Ten days after insisting
scruffy grave diggers did a solemn job
joining mother and daughter together,
you phoned with pauses enough for cancer.

Upset, she described your day as terrible.
Found a masseur in an advert
to ease the knot in your neck,
a constant poking, without rest.

After a cancellation because of the funeral
you waited with her friend in a new salon.
Jolted by the masseur's older appearance
when she asked you to come through.

It was a stern voice that asked
'Any problems I should know about?'
'My mam died 10 days ago
I don't know if it is just tension or an injury.'

An awkward silence stayed, as hands squeezed
and turned muscles. You asked about her work
with dying patients. The lack of engagement
felt like trying to dig over hard earth.

Your neck felt easier. Whatever was crooked
had been straightened. Whatever was trapped
had been set free. The stranger had reached
spaces that you couldn't have found on her own.

V

The woman said 'I hope you don't
mind me asking but who is Tom?'
Not the most obvious question to ask.
You replied 'That was my father's name.'

She said 'Tom's spirit is here now
and he wants me to tell you
he has found your mother again
and you don't need to worry.'

Something burst inside.
The woman pleaded 'Don't cry.
He doesn't want you to be upset.'

She hesitated:
'Does the name Jo, or Joan,
mean anything to you?' You said 'Yes,
it is the name of my little sister who died.'

'Well, she is with them.
The three of them
are all together again
and you don't need to worry.'

In the car you interrogated your friend.
Might she have said something to the woman?
'In the end, I don't care. It is just the way it is.'

Something More

A Different Priesthood

Hanging on a wardrobe door
the bodiless cassock and collar
of a student called to
'Leave all you have and follow me.'

Beneath the black cassock of the night,
flecks of white sea clashed with rocks.
A battling wind threw spears of rain
against the window pane and shook
a locked door on its hinges.

In the chapel
the Prior's bell began Morning Prayer.
'Lord, you know my heart…'
'Like the deer that yearns for flowing water
so my soul is yearning for you, my God.'

I lived with the Carmelites,
where the only warmth,
in the chapel
a candle flickering
beside a draped tabernacle,
beckoning late night visits
to sit awhile and read Isaiah.

I felt a pull from outside
the cold solitudes of medieval ritual,
to walk the cliff paths
among wild garlic and bluebells
prayers in the murmur of the waves below.

A different way
lay in an old bookshop,
in the pages of Rozewicz
who left traditional form
for his heart to walk
the cliff top paths of free verse.

I found it after fourteen years
like a death card in a prayer book.
His book is opened
as often as the Bible
for late night vigils
on a different world
of children asleep.

The sudden sound of coughing
dismisses visions of Wales
calls for a late night visit
to a half-awake boy
too young for words
disturbed by fears.

Lifted up from the cot
as reverently as the Eucharist,
he puts arms around my neck
as prayerful as Isaiah.

Prayer in a Hard World

A woman stands at the sink
washing up the dishes from breakfast.
The priest before the altar
lifts up the paten and chalice.

Her children might be sat in a class,
her little one playing with sand at nursery.
Her children might have grown and left keys
taking from the house their noises.

Bowls slowly emerge from the warm soapy water,
positioned carefully for the suds to drain.
They seemed baptized, renewed, restored,
plates and mugs rejoicing to be again themselves.

Still and distant,
her warm hands part the bubbles
to make a clearance
to swim alone
away from deadline and obligations.

In search of the soul's song
to a place where prayer belongs.

In the underwater dream world she wants
to be free from the sink and swim
back into childhood, to be open,
to be many things at once

to take a run and dive deep, to glide against
the force, to twist and turn,
a presence filling all things - then to be lifted out
on to the surface restored, renewed: dripping.

A woman stands at the altar
and lifts up the deepest of prayers.

I Descend Frequently

the staircase
of my unremarkable years
to the catacombs
where you have been
dying and rising all my life.

The child in me recalls
kneeling at altars,
offering to big handed Irish priests
glass cruets of water and wine.

I have seen
where you leave a presence
in moments made vulnerable
where eyes plead
to be sheltered:

bathing the sick,
whole body immersed in warm water
a gentle rinse of shampoo
guarding eyes.

Holding the hand of a dying man
joining daughter and father together,
closing the door on their
final moment's intimacy.

Wiping faeces
from stained skin
turned on one side,
humiliation
eased by a gentle whisper.

I suspect
you are always
coming towards me
in me
with me
through me.

Alice in Search of the Kingdom

Like Alice
I fell down through the pages.

I would have listened
and ran for more water
so Mary had enough for your feet.

I would have wanted to help like Simon
with the wood on my shoulder
and against my cheek.

I would have burned inside
as well when listening to you
explain it all on the road to Emmaus.

When I was young
I searched for you
thinking of priesthood,
I stayed in a priest's house alone.
He said I should sleep in his bed.
In the dark he got in beside me.

He didn't grab me,
no bulge of an erection against me.
Before anything happened
I said I wanted to sleep
in the spare bed down the corridor.

Thirty five years later
on the streets of Lourdes
my mother said did I know
that Father so and so was here
and asking to see me.

What would you say?

He was desperate and lonely
hungry for any human contact?

A voice from somewhere spoke
'Fuck that for a laugh
keep well away from him.'

Sometimes I See

when we give beyond the obligated
we become the occupied
in a place outside the ordinary
where the word is made flesh.

Relationships

Marie Fidele i.m.

In the nineteen twenties
through a carriage window
you let go in a glance
your childhood in an ancient chateau,
as the horses
pulled towards
an enclosed convent in Paris.

During the war
young German soldiers
occupying the convent
missing their mothers
looked out for you.

Hidden away in a tomb
of cloistered walls
in the solemn chants
of monastic hours
your ears became accustomed
to someone's whispering steps
making footprints in the sand.

In the stillness
of all night vigils
a sower carrying dreams
opened your eyes
to a new decision
to leave the order for the Pyrenees
and a new life in Lourdes.

. . . .

I, the reluctant boy pilgrim
dragged by a mother to the holy shrines
away from French girls in souvenir shops
met you sitting alone in a kitchen

silently peeling vegetables.
Your disciplined hands
taught me to strip the potato
to its white soul.

In the chapel I knelt beside your profile
and listened to the only sound,
your breathing,
heavy with prayer
crossing the silence to another world.

Your breathing
disappeared and returned
like bare feet
walking on sand,
following the footprints
made by one who had just left
an empty tomb.

I made my pilgrimage many times.
You taught me your aristocratic French
as I laughed at your accent imitating my Scouse.

Then I saw you gone, laid for the earth.
I felt an outer skin emerging.

Now when lost and needing
the refuge of your company
I seek the solitude
of dimly lit churches
where at times I hear your breathing.

A Nemesis of a Kiss

Her lip soaked kiss
wore
no clothes.

I met a woman
I shouldn't have slept with
and I didn't.

So I told the truth
about a lie
I didn't tell.

And was found guilty
of a sin
I didn't commit.

Her kiss undressed
and slept with my lie.

Parent

Mam, How Are Children Made?

A canopy
of a tree in blossom
gives us respite
from the heat
of parenthood.

Having a child
tilts you on a new axis,
expectations greater than
what was given to you.

A child enclosed
between hands
stretches arms
up to petals.

Her hand
pulls to her mouth
our vulnerable
sense of selves.

From our own
incompleteness
condemned to do
what's right
better than our parents.

Too much destroys
as too little.
At times
we see a Frankenstein's
desires
as strong as
six unbroken horses.

Under the canopy
where was the warning?
Our slow regrets
a long time before
absent late night mobile phone calls.

After Arguments an Emptiness

A daughter slams the door behind her
and tries to leave the happier photographs
from along the mantelpiece.

My shoulders try to remember
the last time her arms formed
the tight band of a deliberate embrace.

Amputees complain of phantom limb pain.
I ache in the space
where she used to be.

The Real Adventure is to Find You

Another late night mobile phone vigil-
my presence like a ghost.

When I move to get close
I am a dumb lamb
brought to slaughter
by her tongue.

All I can do
is to find this place -
release into the silence this:

when she was young
we would put the table on four chairs
skirted a blanket to hide the legs.

It became below deck,
a step ladder to climb,
to the stern of our ship
wild sea spray in our faces
her eyes shining,
finger pointing
beyond the walls of the kitchen.

Care

Sharing the Silence

At the end of a shift
a silence descends like falling snow
on this empty changing room
in the depths of a general hospital,

a retreat,
a sanctuary
to pray in

to feel again the grip
around my shoulders of an old man's hands
as I lower him on to a bed,
peeling off his feet, the urine soaked pyjamas,
watched uneasily by eyes glazed with shame.

In the footsteps of a woman in her eighties,
I affirm her efforts
at lifting up her swollen legs,
hands pressing hard
on the bars of a Zimmer frame.
Breathless, each step forward
a victory, leaving behind
the dog-chasing suggestion
of a nursing home.

I guide a spoonful of mince
inside an old man's toothless mouth.
He coughs it back in a splutter
adding to it a white viscous phlegm.
My other hand around his ribs
strains to keep him upright,
as he clears his breath,
feeling the rumble
and high notes of a wheeze
from thirty years with ICI chemicals.

Knelt at the feet
of a woman
lop-sided with a stroke
mouth drooped,
I dry between her toes
under her breasts
between her legs
her skin rice paper thin,
holding in my hands the presence
of something sacred.
Her words come backwards off her tongue.
In her eyes the bewildered look of a child
trying to knock on a door
that is missing.

An anonymous face shifts
from being another patient
to feeling like my mother.
The bone-showing,
sculptured profile
of her face sinks heavily
in the white hospital pillow.

Beneath the sheets
the pressure of her clenched hand
slowly fades and opens
after days of being tight.

Her intermittent breath comes
like waves upon a shore
then the silence waits
for the incoming tide
never to arrive.

Thoughts are squeezed out
by the many eyes
turned towards mine during the shift:
making a bridge for conversations,
inviting me into
their personal stories,
from where I never wholly return.

Leaving Teesside

They call her Elsie.
She married a dock worker
when there weren't any cars
on Stockton's cobbled streets.
Given some wages
but not as much
as the amount that laughed
its way down a pub's urinal,
she suffered the bruises of obedience
for speaking her mind
trying to feed
five of them.

Now in a hospital bed
for the elderly infirm
her withered face
lies on its side
against a pillow.

Her fading breeze
is listened to
by adult sons and daughters
lost in reminiscence.

Her hand outside the sheets
once had the strength
of a blacksmith
when it slapped their heads
demanding the truth
and hammered the table
emphasising what was law
in her house.
Now without force,
held in theirs
to keep,
to prevent her leaving
them without a centre.

They call her Edith,
forever a daughter,
who at seventy
had never left her childhood room.
Never felt somebody else
beside her in bed
warming the sheets.

Sitting in Day Care with other women
who talk about their grandchildren
she knits a speedy rhythm
with the clickety needles,
the growing shapes
of small backs and arms
from balls of wool.

In the day room
she inspects intensely
the nurses' every moves
drawing them closer
into her knitting
for a moment to be made intimate.

When she whispers
you can see
crossing the air
the ghost of a young girl.

The mystery of the vacancy
of her special chair
for a few unexpected days
is solved one morning
by a nurse reading the Gazette
under the column of the lately dead.

They call her Annie
known by all who stepped over her
crouched on her knees
scrubbing the steps
of the doctor's surgery.

Now in her seventies
she arrives in the ambulance
coming weekly to the Day Hospital
her finger pointing in the air
a request without words
for her morning embrace.

There is a feeling
that she might crumble
suddenly in my hands.
I can feel every bone
through her clothes
from the forties.
They would fit
someone twice the size
she is.

Four foot five of a body
that refuses to die.
Voiceless from an earlier stroke.
She can only see
through one animated eye.

In there
she is totally present
bigger than the rest of her.
She is standing on the rim
of her own eyelid
watching, enjoying
all that is going on.

She arrives one morning
fitting in the ambulance
and never recovers
leaving her daughter
at the bed side
looking at herself
in the mirror
of a vacant eye
that refuses to close.

They call her Audrey
who while hanging
out the washing
noticed her hand
began to tremble
from an earthquake called Parkinson's,

wanted to be a recluse
because of the many eyes
that stopped to stare at her shaking.
Having a face without expression
made giggling babies
shy away back to mummy.

In twenty years
she made all the nurses
feel like her family.
She became as close
as a mother for strangers,
knowing the feelings
of being an exile.

She was always seen
with a Zimmer frame
like it was her lifelong wrestling companion.
When she lifted it up
it seemed as if
it was trying
to wriggle away from her.

On a visit to the hospital
an ulcer erupted that wouldn't stop bleeding,
leading her down the corridors of a coma
with nurses watching from the doorway.

Lying still for the first time in years
in the silence
outside the window
two birds
suddenly flew from a branch
up into the sky
as if carrying her between them.

Like the Deer That Yearns for Flowing Water

There is a thought buried in me
like inside of a tomb.
The sun looks trapped
behind dormant trees in the window
above my head laid on this pillow.
The quicksand mood is always pulling on me.

The curtain is dragged back by tired night staff,
vacated eyes where the dead already exist.
I feel the tense indifference that steels the night nurse's grip.
A glance can bring sunlight even in the dark.

He jerks bedclothes off my naked deformed body.
The rhythms in my chest quicken when he is near.
I plead to myself to look apologetic
at where the urine bottle has overflowed.

Angrier thoughts want to roar: Yea I pissed the bed.
What did you expect you lazy bastard? You
put it there at midnight of course it overflowed.
If you didn't sleep and did your work I'd be dry.

He dresses me as you would
a Guy Fawkes's doll in November,
pushes his hand and arm under my crotch,
then the other arm over my shoulder.

Breathe deeper now against the pain
as he hauls me on to his chest.
He bends low, drops me into a wheelchair
just a huge sack of potatoes.

Lying in my wheelchair
in my curtained room
I can see my reflection
like a scan image
in the switched off
belly of the television.

The Lightness of Self

The seam of a scar
on a shaven head
of a young woman.

Arrested whilst
having a clot removed
leaving one side emptied.

Looked at me
as if newly dead, wondering
where she had been.

Her eyes seemed
to see things
as if through water.

Then I witnessed
her surfacing,
into being

vulnerable like the powder
that comes off
butterfly wings

'Hold me.
Be gentle.
Make me safe.'

Quicker than thought
turned in on herself
and descended

to where
we all are
adrift like dust

in sunlight
in the absence
after the words.

The God in All This

'I'll just pass you over'-privacy button bleep.
'It's Joanne her sister-in-law, forty dying of cancer.
Can you speak to her? She's so upset. They've said
the chemo's not working it's just a matter of days.'

'Everyone is just stunned. She has three young children
and no one is talking. She is one of the nicest persons you
could ever hope to meet. Why did this have to happen?
Her mother is so angry asking: where is the God in all this?'

On another day in a quiet room off the corridor of a busy ward
I talk to relatives. This comes out in to the room.

'You're the only one who has told us our mam's going to die.
We'll have to put all this pain on hold and just ensure that
we make the most of the time she has left. Let's make sure
it's as good as it can be. We'll have to just go beyond ourselves.'

Dying

Charon the Ferryman

Have you any thoughts
about why you were
admitted in hospital?

I sense the meaning
of my question
reach him,
like a jolt of adrenaline
from going through
a red light accidentally.

He knows,
standing at the door of the plane
looking down
soon he must jump
without a chute.

It's cancer isn't it?
I'm going to die?
How long do you
give me?

Everything he ever did
does not prepare him
for this doorway.

He wasn't here once.
Pondering now,
all he has become
all he has done
all he should have done.

What's it going be like?
I've still hedges to cut,
things to put in order.
The hardest things
are being a burden,
and leaving the family.

Are you able to talk
with them?

I'd rather we stopped

talking now.

Am I Dying?

Your hesitancy
makes me leak
in places I cannot reach.

I feel
the screek of ice
under my feet
wondering how quickly
it's going to give way.

My question
has opened a place
more intimate than sex.

We Die Untidy Deaths

In a hospice
in-patient room,

rolled out,
the tapestry of his life
in conversation.

Worked oil
in Nigeria and Aberdeen.

I need more time
probably to make
more mistakes.

Showed me
a photograph album
of himself
working in a dozen countries.

Wife and daughter empty
ready to be emptied again
silent in the far corner of the room.

The Truth About Hospitals

Nurses try to avoid
the place where they are invited
to listen to

Am I going to die?

You haven't become enough
until you can occupy
the emptied space
you have to leave.

Stronger Than You Thought

I asked you *what's the worst thing about dying?*

You hesitated before stepping off, eyes closed,
the highest diving board in the swimming pool.

Instead of the expected answer

you dropped through
not seeing your daughter in her wedding dress
the world turning without you
your birthday not remembered.

The impact on my kids.

Death Has a Way With Words

'I dread these conversations.
I feel so helpless.
Too clinical: she'll think I don't care.
Too casual: I'll put my foot in it.
I don't want her feeling worse
after talking to me.
She's examining me
in the corner of my eye.'

'But doctor, we know what she's like.
She's not as strong as she pretends.
Anyway, who gives you the right
to take away all her hope?
She'll turn her head to the wall
and just give up on us,
and where will you be
in the middle of the night
when we are left alone?
You can't tell our mam the truth.'

'While he was telling me
I just kept thinking
he's just a bairn.
How awful for him
to have to tell me
my bad news.'

The Ward Buzzer Squeals Without Sympathy

Easing the door inwards
her head turns slowly
her eyes as open as a front door
inviting you into a life full with family.

The cancer flicks away.
The chemotherapy
drains her energy.
Even sentences
feel too heavy to lift.

She's more concerned
about the emptiness
her abrupt leaving
might cause in others.

I'm going to miss my daughter
and the grandchildren the most.

I don't want to be a burden on her
I just want it over
I wish I was gone.

We discuss the importance
of finishing a good story.
The way in which
things come together
lives on in us.

She looks up
as if a thought
walked through walls,
together with the daughter
sorting out the jewellery
suitcase opened
on her bed at home
choosing her best clothes
for charity shops.

When I Die the Dead Will Have Their Say

Whenever I was a vessel
for sweet wine to be tasted
wonderful moments occurred.

Whenever I was the wine
of my own importance
ego spilled over the patients.

The constant prayer:
something in today's encounters
will have more meaning than others
help me be open to the pull of heaven.

I learned how we die:
the changes to the colour of our complexion,
the way the breathing ebbs and flows
towards the end, ramblings from some about
seeing their own dead coming to collect them.

It became a fine art of recognising.
I used to bring families back
away from their cars
back to the bedside
for those last precious moments.

I don't do it any more.

I dreamt I died and went to heaven
and some of the dead I'd cared for
were in a queue
wanting to speak to me.

Shall we tell you
the way it was for us?

We knew we were going.
It was distressing to see the family
trying to keep us here.
We could hear their pain
in quiet conversations.

We were all looking for
any half opportunity
to go without a fuss
not wanting to get undressed in public.

So when they told you:
We need a break.
Home for an hour.
Outside for a smoke.

We thought hallelujah
we'll go.

Then the door opened.

Fuck! You brought them all back again.

Biography

Mel McEvoy was born in Liverpool in 1959. Spent a period of time in religious life. Lived in the North East since 1982. A nurse for 30 years. A specialist in palliative and end of life care. Uses poetry in clinical education. One of the first editors of Teesside's 'Outlet' magazine. Member of poetrycircle.com. He lives in Darlington.